FEDERAL INNOVATION:

You and New Agriculture

Francis W. Wolek

Professor Emeritus

Villanova University

Palantine Books

Audubon, Pennsylvania

2015

Federal Innovation: You and New Agriculture

First edition printed 2015 in the United States

ISBN 13:9781522949848

Library of Congress Control No.:

Cover Graphic: Licensed from iStock Image No. 235446403

For information on this book, please email:
www.francis.wolek@villanova.edu

i

TABLE OF CONTENTS

PREFACE

I'm a true believer! I believe that investments in people, technology, and infrastructure pay off for all of us. I believe people try their best to contribute and help others. In short, I believe a positive outlook is needed through life.

Furthermore, I never give up on others or on my positive outlook. Nowhere else is this more true than on technology. Thus, a recent book advocates a positive stance on cooperative R&D despite a nosedive in cooperative innovation in past years. Of top 10 consortia in 1975, many prestigious, only two remain in existence.

Current society may make different judgements than I. But I'm not giving up. Indeed, I bet investments in the future such as in R&D will emerge again. When they do, people should not simply return to what they did. They should from past successes and mistakes and do a better job. That's why I'm writing books to guide the return to positive thinking and faith in science and technology.

Another inheritance from my origins is that I genuinely like people! Not just in the ideal but all of human reality. Thus, my research is based on real cases of real people struggling with real technologies. This is not the orientation of all academics. So, my books are not filled with quotes and citations. Indeed, my data and conclusions are an outlier from those of colleagues I respect and from whom I've learned.

Frank Wolek

Audubon, PA

2015

SUCCESS STORIES

Public faith in the future is anchored in the talent and creativity of America's scientists and engineers. That faith exists despite belief that government can't innovate. Understanding and acting in markets just seems beyond public servants.

So why are leaders so positive about federal innovation? A 2011 Presidential Memorandum states: "[A] driver of successful innovation is technology transfer ... [so, we must] adapt Federal research for ... the marketplace." Congress seconds this with some eight Innovation Acts proclaiming the value of federal R&D. This chapter shows that this faith in federal innovation is valid and that investment in government labs does make sense!

Economists tell us that federal investment is warranted only when markets fail to innovate. One such context is large, diverse markets of small buyers; markets like agriculture. Millions of farmers produce many different crops on different kinds of farms. Perception of market failure here was so widespread that organized an Agricultural Research Service (ARS) in 1953. Chapter 2 shows that market failures do justify ARS.

Chapter 3 outlines a chief reason for ARS's successes: they emerge from Innovation Communities. This study shows that: 1) these communities are fragile, 2) learning from their past success is not an easy matter, and 3) investing in communities is excellent public policy.

Success? Says Who and Why?

This book is anchored on case projects from the mid-1980s that leaders believed successful. Industry and ARS nominated an equal number of cases that: work in practice and pay off for companies,

1

farmers, and the public. ARS's nominations came from 26 large labs with over eight scientists (see Exhibit 1). An equal number of cases came from the Research Chairs of industrial associations (see Exhibit 2). By the way, for the sake of simplicity, all professionals here are called scientists.

Forty-nine (49) complete cases were obtained and a majority (61%) was successfully transferred into practice. These results jibe with studies of returns from agricultural R&D that show mean returns of 65% per year.

Twenty- three cases involved transfer to companies seeking to develop commercial products. Transfers to suppliers may seem at odds with the common view that ARS produces results transferable to farmers. This may have been true, but is no longer.

An interview guide was developed using the literature on technology transfer. The overall message of that literature is innovations are most successful when pulled into the market by users needing a technology. Such *Market Pull* contrasts with technologies that scientists *Push* into markets. Sure enough, successful cases at ARS exhibit Market Pull.

The cases show that tying technology to needs is so complex and experiential that face-to-face interaction is needed. ARS's scientists must interact with companies and farmers "on-site," where prototypes are tested. Decisions on the design of prototypes and trials; measures of outcome, and future plans must be made through interactive cooperation. Not only did 83% of successful cases show such interaction, but only 16% of cases were successful when it didn't occur.

Table 1

1984 LAB SURVEY

LABORATORY	LOCATION	# SCIENTISTS
National Bee Research	Tucson, AZ	8
National Tillage Machinery	Auburn, AL	8
Arthropod Borne Disease	Denver, CO	9
Tobacco Research	Oxford, NC	9
Northern Grain Insect Laboratory	Brookings, SD	10
Southern Agricultural Energy	Tifton, CA	10
Southeast Watershed	Tifton.GA	10
South East Fruit & Nut	Byron, GA	11
Citrus Laboratory	Winterhaven, FL	12
Field Crop Insect	Stoneville, MS	12
Southeast Poultry	Athena, GA	12
Vegetable Research	Charleston, SC	12
Grassland Soil & Water	Temple, TX	13
Northern Great Plains	Mandan, ND	13
Sugar Cane Field Lab	Houma, LA	13
Plant Science Research	Stillwater, OK	14
Yakima Agricultural Research	Yakima, WA	14
Conservation & Production	Bushland, TX	15
Human Nutrition Laboratory	Grand Forks, ND	15
Pasture Research	University Park, PA	15
Water Conservation	Phoenix, AZ	15

Table 1 (Cont.)

National Animal Disease	Ames, IA	61
Plant Physiology Institute	Beltsville, MD	62

Table 1 (Cont.)

Animal Science Institute	Beltsville, MD	63
Plant Protection Institute	Beltsville, MD	64
Human Nutrition Research	Beltsville, MD	69
Agric. Environment Institute	Beltsville, MD	84
Southern Research Center	New Orleans, LA.	125
Eastern Research Center	Wyndmoor, PA	148
Western Research Center	Berkley, CA	149
North Central Center	Peoria, IL	161

Exhibit 2
ORGANIZATIONS SURVEYED

COMMODITY CENTERED

ARS	INDUSTRY

Plant Commodities

ARS	INDUSTRY
Tobacco Research (NC)	National Potato Foundation
Southeast Fruit & Nut (GA)	Nat'l Grain & Feed Association
Vegetable Research (SC)	Florida Citrus Nursery Growers
Irrigated Agriculture Res. (OR)	Nat'l Assoc. of Wheat Growers
Horticultural Laboratory (FL)	Horticultural Research Institute
Grain Marketing (KS)	National Sunflower Association
Horticultural Institute (MD)	American Soybean Association
North Central Center (IL)	Am. Textile Manufacturing Inst.
Western Center (CA)	Quaker Oats Company
Southern Center (LA)	Reynolds Tobacco Company

Animal Commodities

ARS	INDUSTRY
Southeast Poultry (GA)	Poultry & Egg Institute of Amer.
Meat Animal Research (NB)	Meat Institute
Animal Science Institute (MD)	National Pork Producers Council
Eastern Center (PA)	National Cattlemen's Association

HEALTH CENTERED

Animal Health

ARS	INDUSTRY
Veterinary & Toxicology (TX)	U.S. Animal Health Association
Arthropod Borne Disease (CO	Livestock Conservation Inst.
Nat'l Animal Disease Ctr. (IA)	Upjohn Company

Insect Control

ARS	INDUSTRY
Yakima Agricultural Res. (WA	Assoc. of App. Insect Ecologists

Livestock Insect (TX)	Amer. Mosquito Control Assoc.
	Exhibit 2 (Cont.)
Insect Attractants (FL)	Nat'l Agric. Chemists Assoc.
Insects Affecting Man (FL)	Abbott Laboratories Assoc.

RESOURCE CENTERED
_____

Water Resources

Water Conservation (AZ)	Irrigation Equip. Mfg. Assoc.
Salinity Laboratory (CA)	Am. Water Resources Assoc.
Water Quality (OK)	

Other Resources

Pasture Research (PA)	Nat'l Assoc. Conserve. Districts
Northern Great Plains (ND)	Amer. Forage & Grass Council

GEN'L & BASIC AREAS
_____

Plant Genetics Institute (MD)	Assoc. Official Agric. Chemists
Plant Protection Institute (MD	Animal Breeders Assoc.
Plant Physiology Institute MD	Farm Equip. Producers Assoc.
Agric. Environ. Institute (MD)	Amer. Seed Trade Assoc.
Richard Russell Center (GA)	Institute of Food Technologists
Metabolism & Radiation (SD)	Alice Farms Corp.

Cooperation Doesn't Just Happen

OK, just put people together and make sure they talk to one another. Simple eh? Not really! First, adopters must need to change. Power steering was not adopted until 25 years after its invention because there wasn't a need until then. Fifty years of improvement on horseshoes didn't slow until 1915 when buyers switched to automobiles.

OK; be sure adopters aren't absorbed in another technology. Sorry again. Preparation takes more than an obvious need. The need behind the success of many technologies was not foreseen by developers. Inventors of the radio thought they were working on faster news communication. But the need that fueled growth was ship-to-shore communication.

Regardless of people's skill and the trust between them, definition of need is not possible until the technology is used. Realistic trials and adopter understanding is needed for adoption. William Kelly, an American, England's Henry Bessemer independently discovered how to make steel. Kelly was quickly forgotten but Bessemer won world-wide recognition. The difference? Kelly never explained the technology while Bessemer made the process understandable and even wrote a paper for a British scientific society.

The point is that new technology has to be related to adopter thinking. For this to happen, adopters as well as scientists must understand the logic of present and proposed methods. The task is to: 1) relate a new method to adopter need, 2), be different from existing methods yet, 3) meaningful to production and market conditions.

And we're not finished yet. Patterns of thinking, the cognitive styles, of adopters and technologists differ. Scientists parse problems into variables linked by linear logic. Managers rely on an intuitive feel for the whole situation. For example, an ARS scientist couldn't understand why industrialists weren't interested in a new way to prove varietal origins of plants. The method was not only elegant but used cutting edge technology. For their part, managers wanted to grasp how the technology solved a problem.

The Work of Cooperation is Adaptation

An eighty-three percent success rate is nothing to sneeze at! In fact, it's downright suspicious. The Swedes discovered how risky innovation is when making awards for inventions. Out of 2,700 entries, only 10 (0.4%) were commercially attractive. A U.S. program on energy inventions found a similar 0.3% rate on forecasted rates of profit and energy savings.

Successful cases show that interaction can yield valuable adaptation. Unforeseen circumstances jeopardize innovations. The saving factor here was the interaction of scientists and adopters. When difficulties arose, projects were adapted to overcome them; people did what was necessary for success!

A new insect control technology was stymied by unexpected difficulty in scaling up production to commercial quantities. A promising technology was about to become brilliant, but impractical science. Instead, industry developed a new process. Good science became good business. Also true, scientists gained valuable insight into the molecular dynamics of the attractant.

The cases here were pre-screened to be good science from investigators at the top of their professions. So, why couldn't the scientists adapt to unexpected problems? At least part of the answer is that scientists failed to see and understand market and production factors. For example, a technology for fixing nitrogen worked fine in the lab. But marketers said it offered insufficient benefit to farmers to justify costs of production and marketing. The result was good science and no impact. Just as bad, lab managers judged the science as not worth further research.

On their own, government scientists lack the experience to anticipate problems and opportunities in commerce. In seven of

9

the ten cases, failure occurred because the technology did not satisfy a sufficiently strong need for users to change practice. For example, one scientist developed a way to control unwanted plant growth and maximize product growth. After publication, market experts found there was no American producer for the machinery and farmers lacked the capital needed to change practice.

INTERACTIVE COMMUNITIES

We've seen that when ARS scientists actively interact with users, their ideas lead to successful innovation. Without interaction, there can be waste, frustration, and little or no application.

The Informal Communities of Agriculture

Some managers may argue that laboratory directors should require interaction with users. Others might suggest that be encouraged to interact. However, the most impressive characteristic of successful transfers at ARS is that screening and interaction were quite informal.

For example, the variety NC82 of tobacco is resistant to bacterial wilt, is easily cured, and became the most popular flue-cured tobacco developed by ARS. The informal interaction on NC82 was through the New Variety Advisory Group of the Tobacco Yorkers Conference; which takes great pains to retain its informality. The Conference has no charter, formal process, or central authority. However, state agencies with authority will not act (register, authorize breeding seed, disseminate information, etc.) on a variety without a conference consensus approval.

The way in which an advisory group reaches consensus on approval is a model of collegiality. New varieties are discussed at the group's convention. A vote is taken but only after consensus is evident on such issues as:

a. Do field and laboratory tests show the variety passes minimums (nicotine, sugar content, ·appearance, etc.) needed for buyer interest?

b. Have experimental plantings generated sufficient interest among farmers and buyers?

c. Have sufficient data been obtained on advantages, problems, and management (e.g., sucker control)?

d. Is the variety necessary given the availability of others and pressures on farmers to make other investments?

ARS takes a consensus to wait or to drop further work seriously. In every case, emphasis is on consensus that serves the public, producers and the market. It is generally true that the consensus is influenced by the research of a senior ARS scientist-breeder. Some might argue that ARS should not influence application. However, both the community and the culture of ARS argues against this:

a. History shows new science emerges from application as well as new applications emerge from science.

b. Ideas for application and science are frequent by-products of interaction.

c. Crises in agriculture (e.g., diseases, shortages, barriers, etc.) require ARS expertise unavailable elsewhere.

d. ARS scientists are dedicated to progress in agriculture and seeing their work have practical impact.

ARS Transfer Agents: Some have suggested that ARS establish an in-house corps of Transfer Agents. Agents could provide such assistance as: (1) facilitating contacts with industry; (2) providing a clearinghouse for the public and the press and (3) serving as advisors on patents, licenses, and dissemination.

Transfer staffs make sense for work on such formal matters such as patents and cooperative agreements (CRADAs). Indeed, studies have found that some scientists resist involvement in commercial activities. Others say the main reason they work on such activities is "because they are told to do so." Nevertheless, cases show that scientists have primary role because:

a. The reputation of scientists attracts attention to and confidence in discoveries (e.g., a test method for food toxins requires a grasp of microbiology).

b. Practical use of technology involves scientific issues that only scientists can explain (e.g., a water conservation system for water districts with widely different needs).

c. The reputation of scientists is critical to confidence in results (e.g., a new vaccine replacing an inexpensive product that has regulatory problems).

d. It is impossible to predict interest and results (e.g., a market for a biological insect control originated by chance during a visit on another subject).

e. The energy and enthusiasm of scientists is impossible to replace with agents (e.g., a test for varietal integrity that was a life-long dream of the scientist involved).

f. Industry is reluctant to deal with other intermediaries (e.g., a study that established equipment standards for worker health and safety).

The dominant goal of ARS is and will continue to be scientific progress. New science can be an outgrowth of questions and problems from the field. Scientists are best positioned to be aware of and to assess such opportunities. NASA and other agencies with transfer staffs have reduced technologies to practical form for their own missions.

An issue arises on basic research outcomes. Where can interaction be focused on fundamental insights into complex fields such as molecular biology? A common finding in transfer studies is that the more basic the science, the more complex the "translations" to practice. Such translation requires not only extensive interaction, but qualifications for mutual understanding. In other words, it takes a scientist to understand science.

Where do scientist users come from? Who has a background to understand both basic results and an identity with commerce to bridge gaps to practice? The majority of such people are in the laboratories of large companies. In other words, as ARS becomes more involved in basic research, it may encounter the danger of applications becoming dependent on large corporations.

A System of Informal Interaction

If interaction is so central, why don't scientists demand support? A partial answer is in cases where scientists focus on adopters with whom interaction was easy. This bias is not necessarily poor practice. Companies as well as ARS have shared responsibility for transfer. Balance is needed, but companies that take initiative on ties deserve closer relationships.

In other words, the system providing interaction must be informal and based on judgment, connections, and scientific competence. Excellent results ensue, but no system will insure systematic and open access. However, a basic conflict may need addressing. On the one hand, an informal culture is nurtured by common commitment to agriculture. On the other hand, policy encourages individual brilliance. The first system takes pride in interaction. The second takes pride in personal achievement.

The Importance of Interaction to Innovation

Is the importance of interaction an enduring essential? This is especially relevant since cases are from the mid-1980s. So, let's examine the extent of interaction in industry. After all, didn't Edison invent technologies on his own? While a full answer would take a book, we'll briefly examine technology from the last hundred years or so. For starters, Edison's name appeared on all patents but he had many collaborators; a group so large they proudly organized as "Edison Pioneers."

In fact, industrial history is replete with examples of fruitful interaction that was both unexpected and difficult to manage. The lesson: building and managing transfer communities is basic.

Figure 1 Edison Pioneers

Petroleum Refining: The first process for processing crude, the Burton Process, was developed by a team at Standard Oil of Indiana. Being chemists, the team naturally thought of batch processes. Edgar Clark, trained as a chemical engineer, focused on continuous processes. The team unexpectedly faced and overcame this cognitive difference and developed Fluid Catalytic Cracking.

15

But, this could not have happened if Clark's contributions to the batch process had not justified acceptance in the community.

Radio: Guglielmo Marconi was focused on mechanisms of radio and inexperienced in instrument construction. Following an unexpected introduction to William Preece, head of the British Post Office, skilled Office mechanics made radio components. Later mistrust generated by Marconi's secrecy on American financing and Preece's about German observers disrupted the sense of community and impacted transfer.

DC-3 Air Transport: Cyrus Smith, American Airline's CEO, flew the DC-2 wanted a plane for a New York to Chicago flight non-stop. Douglas was reluctant to do yet another design, but an unexpected call from Smith convinced him to modify the DC-2 into a sleeper. A transfer community emerged when Douglas technicians united with American experts on market know-how. Where did Smith get the money Douglas needed? Smith tapped a Federal fund appropriated for depression recovery.

So far the message is that innovative interaction was not and could not be formalized. A different story examines international developments that emerge over a hundred years. A story that is common in history and occurred on the elevator, tractor, light bulb, washing machine among others.

Sewing Machine: Thomas Saint first developed a machine in England in 1790. Many small improvements followed from many countries. The familiar sewing machine, designed by American Isaac Singer, emerged in the mid-1800s when he made a new system from a convergence of the improvements. An unexpected suit on patent violation forced Singer and his attorneys to become experts on industrial organization. The result, a four company Sewing Machine Combination, cornered markets until 1877 when patents expired. International interaction within a diverse community refined the Combination's technology.

Integrated Pest Management: International progress on IPM also took place for over a hundred years before the concept of Integrated Control combined with Pest Management. Just as with the sewing machine, many improvements occurred in a technical community that included ARS (virus carrying nematodes) facilitating organizational leadership. Just as sewing combines interacted with unions to overcome threatened workers, so USDA interacted with threatened pest control contractors.

Some scholars of technology history argue that corporate increasingly dominates technology development and transfer. To the extent that this argument is true, the declining uniqueness of ARS may require more formalized structures for technology transfer. This brief examination suggests that new systems of technology will continue to emerge from interactive communities. Thus, federal labs like ARS will continue to be vital allies of corporations and other organized powers on technologies that restructure science and society.

WAS FED ACTION NECESSARY?

ARS has been in existence for a long time. It grew with US agriculture and state land grants and became a central element of agriculture in the U.S. A key to its success was forsaking the discipline-oriented structure of universities and embracing a problem and commodity-based structure. Success on the likes of soil fertility and hybrid corn encouraged adopters to defer to the good judgment of ARS scientists. If those scientists didn't see a need for interaction, adopters accept it as unnecessary.

Is ARS Unique?

ARS scientists often share common backgrounds: raised on farms and educated at state land-grant universities. They share a love of agriculture and a commitment to its progress. They understand that rural communities prosper by sharing resources, information, and experience. They are products of communities where they learned to work, play, and face life together. From 4H to Grange to Coop they learned that communities accomplish more than individuals. In other words, they are well prepared to rely on interactive communities to promote commercializations.

ARS is aware that its uniqueness may not endure. Agriculture is becoming big business, family farms are decreasing, and basic science is growing. These changes are affecting ARS's culture by decreasing staff raised on farms; increasing organization pressure on communities; and increasing needs for genetics, digitization of information, and computer processing of large databases.

Federal Projects in Agriculture

Although Interactive Communities appear basic to innovation of all kinds, we need to ask if the uniqueness of ARS influences its position as a model of federal action. Economists gave us a way to address with theory arguing that government R&D is warranted only when markets fail to develop socially valuable technology. We'll examine how well market failure characterizes ARS's work. To do this the cases are divided into four types: a) *New Varieties*, b) *Technical Services*, c) *Local Solutions*, and d) *Technology Ventures*:

New Varieties: These cases demonstrate the following market failures: 1) new varieties take too long for private action, and 2) new varieties produce in a wide range of growing conditions. The Lee Soybean took ARS 31 years to develop and field work was needed on different types of farms, soil, and climate conditions.

Seven complete cases were successfully adopted. All seven were: a) responses to recognized needs, b) initiated by a veteran ARS scientist, c) involved field trials by farmers, and d) were disseminated by Interactive Communities.

Variety development requires many years and social and managerial processes emerge for evaluation, field tests, market promotion, and dissemination. Indeed, ARS scientists are able to achieve prominence in the Interactive Communities that emerge such as the Tobacco Workers Conference.

Technical Services: The justification for these projects is that ARS performs a service that is not otherwise available. An example is ARS service screening for food contaminants using advanced instrumentation and expertise. Market failure was also present in that a majority of cases fulfilled another agency's regulatory mission. Policing and controlling food contamination is the job of federal and state agencies which need ARS's reputation for independence for scientific competence.

Of fifteen Service cases, ten (10) were valuable and five (5) were not. All ten valuable cases clearly involved interaction versus no or incomplete interaction on the other five. ARS scientists on the five non-valued cases claimed interaction was unnecessary as only they possessed needed expertise. Furthermore, industrial sources generally agreed! Despite this perceptions, it was sobering to see cases, such as a mathematical model for food quality, where good science had minimal impact.

Problem Solutions: Eight of nine cases of Problem Solution shared a commitment from another government agency. Most other agencies covered regional conservation or health issues; such as: (1) irrigation, (2) soil conservation, (3) insect control, and (4) water supply. Five cases involved crises (e.g., disease carrying insect invasions) and the market failure was the same as for Service cases: the technology was needed by another government agency.

Every case had definite value in a local community but diffusion to other localities was limited. Local agencies and farmers had significant funds and prestige invested in field tests but their involvement was limited to the existence of a local crisis.

New Ventures: The issue of market failure does not arise on these cases as they are spinoffs from other types of work such as basic research. Twenty such cases concerned either: a) animal health (8 cases), b) plant health (7 cases), or c) generic science or technology (5 cases). In short, these cases were outgrowths of scientific work justified for its own sake or by public concern. Nevertheless, most cases were only useful if industry developed the idea into a commercial product and placed it on the market. Farmers may adopt Era Wheat (a Variety case) or use an irrigation system (a Service case). However, Venture cases like the Japanese Beetle Trap require a chemical company to invest in synthesizing and marketing a pheromone in commercial quantities.

Over half the cases (11) were successfully transferred to commercial markets. Transferred cases were usually to new or small companies. Since many of the projects were built on unexpected research results and dealt with technologies outside the interests of established companies (e.g., a new instrument for measuring protein content of forage). Most cases (14) involved no interaction until ARS completed its research and a firm was required for trials. Once commercial work was started, interactive networks were involved in transfer (eight of 11cases).

Implications of the Agricultural Context

Granted that most of ARS's work is warranted, could important types of work also be unwarranted? For sure, ARS, farmers, and agricultural business believe the answer is no and in none but Venture cases did they even raise the question.

Encouragement of Private Services: A justification of market failure is suspect if ARS interferes with market opportunities for for-profit services. ARS is aware of this issue as shown by its history on information services. It developed and disseminated such services when there was little private capability for database services. Now that a large and diversified information industry has the capital, some ARS programs cooperate with information companies. An argument could be made that ARS should also have formal ties to the Information Industries Association and other associations for exploring mutually supportive roles.

Consideration of for-profit technical services will not be easy since many scientists do not recognize the issue. But lab managers should include the issue in project justification since scientific benefits may accrue as well as commercial ones. Commercial services could also assure that market and production factors are part of field tests and this may trigger valuable science..

Will Genetic Engineering be Different? Traditional variety development depends on crossbreeds that are in the same species. The new discipline of Genetic Engineering allows scientists to use a wider search for genes on traits or weaknesses.

Nevertheless, new varieties must go through the same processes of evaluation, field test, market promotion, and variety dissemination as traditional crossbreeds. It is in these processes that Interactive Communities are essential. Genetic Engineering may shorten Variety Development at early stages but still require involvement in community development and operation. If anything, resistance to genetic modification (GMOs) may require more involvement in stronger and more diverse networks.

ARS's strategic plans call for strengthening basic research on plant physiology as well as continuing plant breeding to combat plant disease. An interesting aside is that five of the seven Variety cases focused on market improvements and only two on diseases. The central issue concerns more than ARS breeding; it concerns the communities that guide and facilitate variety development. Can networks with strong ARS ties to communities balance service with the science of basic research?

Encouragement of Inter-regional Transfers: The Problem cases raise an additional question of foregone inter-regional transfers. Local agency personnel are valuable users and have funds and prestige to invest in necessary field tests. However, agency partners do not call for inter-regional transfers unless scientists raise the issue.

MANAGING INTERACTION

We've seen that market failures do inspire federal innovation. But what enables the interaction needed to transfer technology to the marketplace? If knowledge is all that is needed, we could outsource transfer. However: (1) it is impossible to predict interaction needs; (2) technologies, needs, and system configurations develop in constantly shifting patterns; and (3) knowledge and experience is only available in pros. In short, we find that effective interaction must be anchored in individual scientists and commercial experts.

Community-Based Interaction

We've learned that federal scientists are committed to working in Interactive Communities. This requires scientists to: 1) have recognized roles and contributions, 2) be visible in relevant communities, and 3) have experience interacting with multiple parties. They and their adopter colleagues must listen closely and be experienced in Give and Take negotiation. They must understand their organization's goals, have a solid grasp of others' work, and be honestly forthright in Q&A clarification.

Beyond these basics, transfer management will be case specific. Both lab and commercial interests vary in content, transferability, and importance. Managers must exercise judgement, encourage interactive capabilities, and understand when and where outside assistance is needed.

Outside assistance may be needed if internal staff lacks capability or fails to interact. This last possibility occurred in some cases where the need for interaction did not occur to people.

Managers in such cases must convince people to interact or bring in outsiders when they do not.

Interactive transfers occur in most ARS labs. Indeed, some encourage a few scientists to be active publishers to free others to be interaction advisors. When advisers are senior and their involvement transcends specific cases; we are able to say that *Mentoring* is flourishing.

Mentoring is sufficiently important as a social process that some develop regular processes, called protocols, to advise others. For example, suppose, a mentor is involved in transferring a Computer Ground Water Model to a local community. The mentor's protocol might be:

Step 1: Identify a project that would benefit from transfer. Suppose a need exists for a Swine Processing Center.

Step 2: Show how the transfer advances the community. For example, provide statistics on job and tax income growth from centers in similar communities. Also identify odor and effluent controls necessary for satisfaction.

Step 3: List the factors required by the new technology. For example, what are the major aquifers with what measures of flow?

Step 4: Model the system for simulated operation.

Step 5: Map the ground water flows divulged by the model.

Step 6: Translate the map for the user's needs. For example, distribution of odor.

Non-Obvious Principles of Interaction

Adaptive, Informal, and Community-Based Interaction is a complex social process. Indeed, the principles for its management are sufficiently intuitive and contrary to common sense that many professionals fail to appreciate their importance.

Principle of Goal Clarity: Professionals on all sides of the process must be clear and firm on their goals. Scientists need to focus on the steps of exploration (addition of variables, sharpening effects, expanding theoretical relevance, etc.)? Adopters must be clear about their strategy (broadening product line, markets targeted, improving competitive advantage, etc.).

Goal Clarity sets the stage for Q&A sharing of: a) discoveries and their scientific context and b) commercial impact in targeted applications. Each party describes their goals and work in their language and the other listens to understand the basics. Content will vary from project to project, but Question and Answer (Q&A) exchanges are used to assure a basis for the next phase of interaction: a Statement of Needs.

The Dialectic of Stating Needs: A Statement of Needs is where the hard work of interaction takes place since this is where differences emerge in actions, language, and cognitive style. The **Dialectic Method** is designed to deal with these differences. The Method builds on Goal Clarity and requires that:

a. Each party states their needs,

b. Q and A assures understanding of lab and commercial context,

c. Scientists state commercial needs in scientific terms and Adopters state science needs in commercial terms,

d. Via Q&A and reformulation, each party offers Gives and Takes on a Statement of Needs.

e. Each party continues until feasible agreement is reached or a jointly decision it is not possible for stated reasons.

Reformulation is the key step in this Dialectic since this step assures that each party understands the other's goals and needs. This step also provides a common language for interaction. Examples of scientific reformulations of commercial needs are:

a. Variables and ranges for experimentation (reformulation of competitive advantages needed),

a. Volumes, trace specs, and purity targets (reformulation of regulatory clearance requirements),

b. Necessary contextual variables (reformulation of operational requirements),

c. Theoretical anchoring and clarity non-scientific (reformulation of training needs).

Examples of an **adopter's reformulation** of scientific needs are:

a. Customer, Need, and Market Channel specifications (reformulation of theoretical description of phenomenon),

b. Market roll-out plan (reformulation of experimental setup including volume measures, and outcome targets),

c. Production and Usage Process specification (reformulation of contextual variables affecting results),

d. Strategic Context and specification of market impact (reformulation of experimental outcomes defining success and failure).

Windows on the World of Knowledge

Science and technology is constantly evolving via the contributions of organizations around the world. Competent scientists and managers understand their organizations must find, interact with, and encourage a network of these worldwide sources. Both federal and corporate labs become "windows" on this world of relevant knowledge. In fact, scholarly research on technology transfer finds that motivation to establish valuable windows, rather specific transfers, is industry's primary purpose in initiating interaction.

It is important for managers and scientists to understand their organization's status as a "window on the scientific or commercial world." Organizations cannot be a window for all comers on all subjects and their status is achieved and maintained via contributions and contacts at other centers. Managing this status is an important task of managers and individual contributors as it is based on personal contact.

Contextual Knowledge: A corollary of the above is that neither scientists nor commercial firms exist in isolation. An important attribute of projects is relationships to other sources of knowledge. For example, the discussion of Service cases highlighted the importance of information and technical service industries. Not only must labs and consultants interact on service, but must symbiotically support each other. Each must not only provide service, but also assure that their projects positively impact future services for users.

Strategic Transfers

Transfers that have strategic implications are especially important. Examples from this study concern strategies of national programs such as: eradication of boll weevils, digestibility of soy protein, and impacts on water flow (CREAMS). Progress on strategic such transfers requires targeted attention by all parties via regular meetings, reports, and progress summaries. Strategic relevance of projects is also likely to be multi-lateral. For example: a) eradication of the boll weevil was strategically important for USDA and insect control firms, b) digestibility of protein is strategically relevant for food companies and supply chain partners, and c) CREAMS is strategically relevant for USDA, local agencies and rural communities.

Radical Restructuring Projects: Technological progress has two primary modes: 1) **Incremental Improvement** and 2) **Radical Restructuring**. Most transfers are improvements. However, progress occasionally takes a radically new direction; one that restructures knowledge and industries.

Examples of 'blue-sky' restructurings include: a) the Farm of the Future, b) Manufactured Food, and c) Cloned Herds. The Farm of the Future would radically restructure agriculture with computer control of the total process from product selection through the planting-harvesting cycle to distribution. The result would be an integrated process in which computers decide which crops should be raised where and when, how and when they should be nourished, treated, harvested; and how, when, and where produce should be processed and sold. Full data needs would be provided by computer integrated field sensors, market monitors, and integrated databases and processed by total system computer models.

28

The Farm of the Future example illustrates several characteristics highlighted in historical examples of Radical Restructuring. The first is that restructuring commonly results from market driven **Convergences** in existing technologies. For example, the DC-3 Airplane which restructured air transportation was a convergence of several existing lines of improvement (air body streamlining, air-cooled engines, propellers, etc.). Second, restructurings must solve **Common Problems**. For example, restructuring of the electronics industry from vacuum tubes to integrated circuits overcame problems of material impurity in all components. Assurance of consistency in organ and fetus development would have to be assured for Cloned Herds.

In other words, technology transfer on Radical Restructuring requires multiple windows on the world of science and technology. Interaction of scientists and adopters will affect all phases of projects from origin to application. Scientists will be both sources of ideas and learners of new extensions of knowledge. Adopters will be users of information, links to sources of interest, and organizers of progress.

Public Interaction

Interacting with the general public is an important job for scientists and managers. Both must help the public understand problems they are addressing, importance to the public, results the public will experience, and responsibility of the public to maximize positive impacts. Such jobs are often handled by media experts trained in scientific communication. The recommendation here is quite different and demanding for both managers and scientists.

The table below illustrates the use of Dialectic in communication with other parties and with the public. The first column gives a brief title of a project that scientists use with each other. The second column gives a goal statement that speaks to farmers. The third column gives the goal for the public.

Science Title	Farm User Goal	Public Goal
Alfalfa Protein	Crop Value	Water Table Protection
Blue Tongue Serum	Cost Reduction	Meat Improvement
Poultry Cage Design	Cost Reduction	Humane Treatment
Anaerobic Sludge	Regulatory Conform	Odor Reduction
Nitrosamine Meas.	Sales Increase	Grocery Cost
Sire Database	Sire Selection	Meal Selection

###

REFERENCES

Alston, J. M., (2010), "The Benefits from Agricultural Research and Development, Innovation, and Productivity Growth", *OECD Food, Agriculture and Fisheries Papers*, No. 31.

Artz, G., (2003), Rural "Area Brain Drain: Is It a Reality?" *Choices* (Magazine of food and farm issues), 4th Quarter.

Baker, E.C., (1976) *Sir William Preece*, Hutchinson.

Betz, F., (2011), *Managing Technological Innovation: Competitive Advantage from Change*, 3rd Edition, Wiley.

Bozeman, B., (2000), "Technology Transfer Research: A Review and Assessment", *Research Policy*, Vol. 29, pp. 627-655.

Frazier, M. (1997), *A Short History of Pest Management*, 1997, Penn State Extension, http://extension.psu.edu/pests/ipm/

Geisler, E. and Turchetti, G. (2014), "Commercialization of Technological Innovations," *International Journal of Innovation and Technology Management*, Vol. 12.

Holden, H. M., *"The DC-3 Genesis of The Legend,"* http://www.dc3history.org/douglasdc3.html

Kanigel, R., (1986), *Apprentice to Genius: The Making of a Scientific Dynasty*, Macmillan.

National Research Council, (2000), *Genetically Modified Pest-Protected Plants: Science and Regulation,* Committee on Genetically Modified Pest-Protected Plants, Board on Agriculture and Natural Resources.

Maine, E., et al. (2013), "Radical Innovation from the Confluence of Technologies", *Journal of Engineering. Technology. Management.*

Ruttan, V, (2001*), The Role of the Public Sector in Technology Development,* Science, Technology and Innovation Discussion Paper No. 11, Center for International Development, Harvard.

Wikipedia, "Edison Pioneers,"
https://en.wikipedia.org/wiki/Edison_Pioneers

Wikipedia, "Sewing Machine",
https://en.wikipedia.org/wiki/Sewing_machine

About Frank Wolek

My interests and style were strongly influenced by where I was born, raised, and initially educated. I was born in 1935 in Brooklyn, New York; educated in Brooklyn Technical High School, the Colorado School of Mines (Geology), and Harvard Business School (doctorate in the management of science and technology). I've spent most of my career as a Professor of Management at the Wharton School of the University of Pennsylvania and Villanova University (now an Emeritus Professor of Management). My contributions include service as Deputy Assistant Secretary of Science and Technology at the U.S. Department of Commerce and some 75 publications. I am happily married to Gloria Peez Wolek and we are proud of our four children and four grandchildren. I divide my time equally between homes in Florida and Philadelphia.

Other Books by Frank Wolek

Administering Research and Development with Charles Orth and Joseph Bailey, Homewood, IL: Richard D. Irwin, Inc., 1964.

Technology and Information Transfer, with Richard Rosenbloom, Boston, MA: Harvard Business School Division of Research, 1970.

Innovation Policy: Western Provinces of Canada, with Jean Eric Aubert, Francis Bonnet, Michael Proctor, and Veikko Vuorikari, Paris, France: OECD, 1988.

Cooperative Innovation: Key to a New Agriculture, Villanova: Villanova Center for Agricultural Commerce, 1989.

Operations Management, with Matthew Liberatore and Robert Nydick, Villanova, PA.: LNW Publishing, 1998.

R&D Consortia: A Benchmark Study, (ebook), https://www.smashwords.com/books/search?query=Wolek

R&D Consortia: A Benchmark Study, (Paperback), http://www.amazon.com/R-D-Consortia-Benchmark-Study/

Other publications are available through Researchgate at: https://www.researchgate.net/profile/Francis_Wolek

Staying In Touch with Frank Wolek

Linkedin:https://www.linkedin.com/pub/frank-wolek/50/32b/304

Webpage: http://www39.homepage.villanova.edu/francis.wolek/

www.ingramcontent.com/pod-product-compliance
Lightning Source LLC
Chambersburg PA
CBHW061233180526
45170CB00003B/1283